Monkey Business

BABOONS

Gillian Gosman

PowerKiDS press
New York

Published in 2012 by The Rosen Publishing Group, Inc.
29 East 21st Street, New York, NY 10010

Copyright © 2012 by The Rosen Publishing Group, Inc.

All rights reserved. No part of this book may be reproduced in any form without permission in writing from the publisher, except by a reviewer.

First Edition

Editor: Jennifer Way
Book Design: Kate Laczynski

Photo Credits: Cover, pp. 1, 9 Peter Chadwick/Getty Images; pp. 4, 6, 10, 14, 19 iStockphoto/Thinkstock; pp. 5, 7 (left), 8, 11 (left, right), 18 Shutterstock.com; p. 7 (right) James Hager/Getty Images; pp. 12, 17 Hemera/Thinkstock; p. 13 (left) © www.iStockphoto.com/Scott Harms; p. 13 (right) Paula Bronstein/Getty Images; p. 15 Nigel Dennis/Getty Images; p. 16 Sune Wendelboe/Getty Images; p. 20 © www.iStockphoto.com/Gabriela Schaufelberger; p. 21 (left) John Brown/Getty Images; p. 21 (right) Anup Shah/Getty Images; p. 22 Russell Johnson/Getty Images.

Library of Congress Cataloging-in-Publication Data

Gosman, Gillian.
 Baboons / by Gillian Gosman. — 1st ed.
   p. cm. — (Monkey business)
Includes index.
ISBN 978-1-4488-5022-8 (library binding) — ISBN 978-1-4488-5177-5 (pbk.) — ISBN 978-1-4488-5178-2 (6-pack)
1. Baboons—Juvenile literature. I. Title.
QL737.P93G67 2012
599.8'65—dc22

2011003127

Manufactured in the United States of America

CPSIA Compliance Information: Batch #WS11PK: For Further Information contact Rosen Publishing, New York, New York at 1-800-237-9932

Contents

Meet the Baboon 4

Baboon Species 6

Old World Monkeys 8

Where Baboons Live 10

What Baboons Eat.. 12

In the Troop.. 14

Monkeying Around 16

Males and Females 18

Baby Baboons 20

Baboons and People 22

Glossary 23

Index.. 24

Web Sites.. 24

MEET THE BABOON

Baboons, like the one shown here, are closely related to three other kinds of monkeys. They are drills, mandrills, and geladas.

Meet the baboon. The baboon is one of the largest monkeys in the world. Baboons march across grassy plains in groups called troops. They are social animals that show a wide range of behaviors. Baboons may growl and show their teeth to one another when they are ready for a fight. Baboons may also spend quiet time with one another to help build relationships within the troop.

Baboons often travel as a larger troop and break into pairs or small groups when resting.

Like other **primates**, this powerful monkey is a close relative of people. Studying the baboon can teach us more about this monkey as well as its place in the habitats in which it lives. This book will show you more about this amazing monkey.

BABOON SPECIES

There are five **species**, or kinds, of baboons. All five species have some things in common. They are all large and strong. Their fur is brownish gray, red, yellow, or greenish in color. Their faces, the palms of their hands, and the bottoms of their feet are hairless. They have large, tough-skinned, hairless bottoms. These make it easy for them to sit on tree branches or hard ground.

Here you can see the hairless bottom on this baboon. On some baboons, this padding is reddish.

Baboons have long doglike muzzles. A muzzle is the part of an animal's body that includes its mouth and nose. Their eyes are set close together. Baboons have sharp **canines**. When they feel they are in danger, they growl, bark, and show these teeth.

Male hamadryas baboons have puffy, silverish manes of fur around their faces.

This chacma baboon is showing its canines.

OLD WORLD MONKEYS

Baboons are called **Old World** monkeys. Old World monkeys are found in parts of Africa, Asia, and the Middle East. Baboons live in Africa and in the Middle East on the Arabian Peninsula. **New World** monkeys are found in Central America and South America.

Old World monkeys share certain traits. Like other Old

Unlike New World monkeys, baboons cannot use their tails to hold on to tree branches. This is a chacma baboon, a species that lives in southern Africa.

World monkeys, baboons' tails cannot grip things, as many New World monkeys' tails can. Like most other Old World monkeys, baboons have **opposable** thumbs. Baboons' thumbs are longer and stronger than those of most other Old World monkeys, though. Baboons can use their thumbs to grip objects and use them as tools.

This young chacma baboon has used its opposable thumbs to help it pick and eat fruit.

WHERE BABOONS LIVE

Baboons live across central Africa, from Guinea in the west, through Nigeria, Chad, Sudan, Eritrea, and Ethiopia, to Somalia in the east. They also live in the Middle Eastern countries of Yemen and Saudi Arabia. Baboons are also found in the southern African countries of South Africa, Angola, Zambia, and Mozambique.

Guinea, chacma, yellow, and olive baboons are called the

The olive baboon lives in more than 25 countries across central Africa. It is the most widespread of the baboon species.

savanna baboons. They live in hot, dry savannas and grasslands. Olive baboons also live in hot, wet **tropical** forests. The hamadryas baboon lives among the cliffs on the African and Middle Eastern shores of the Red Sea.

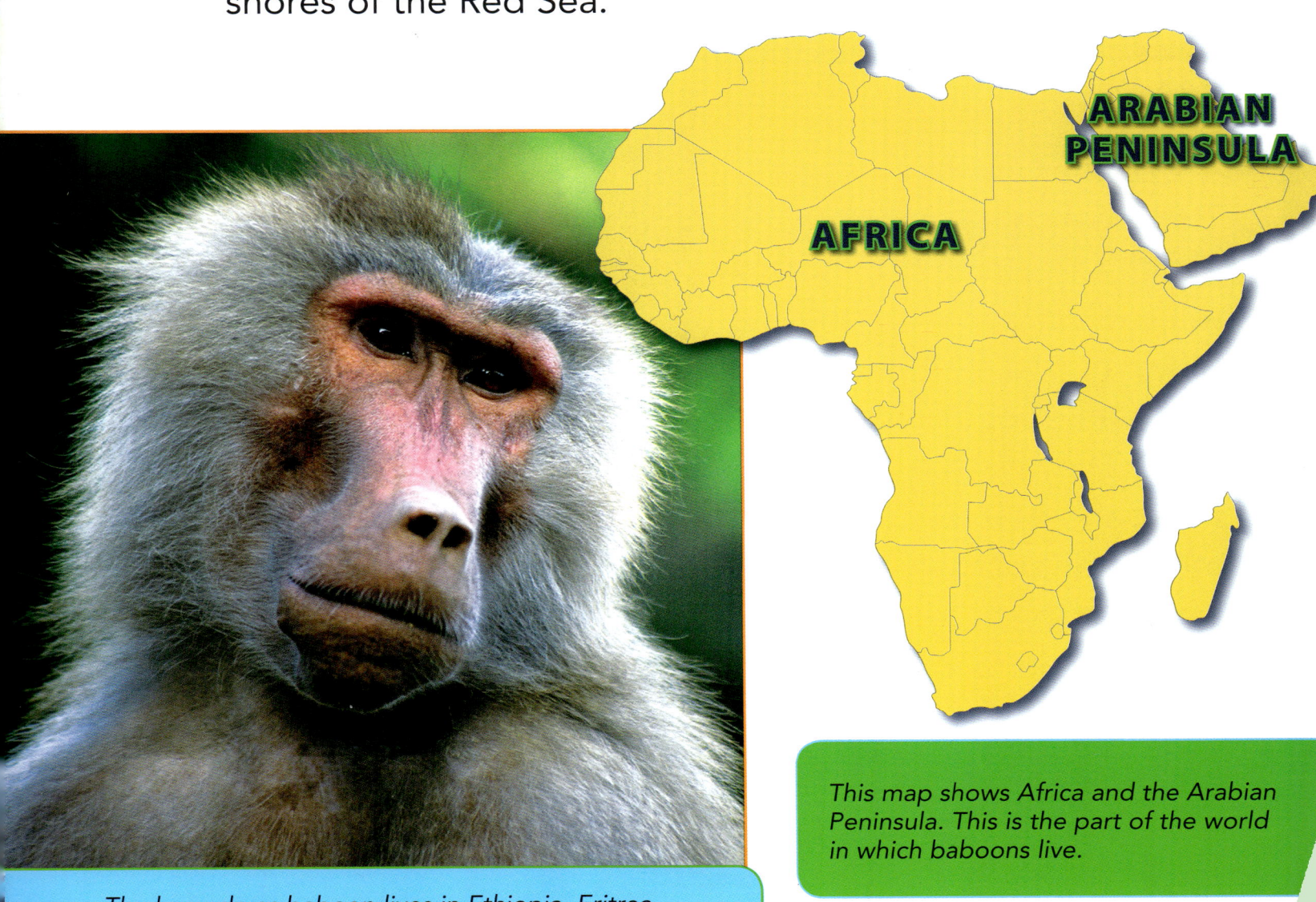

This map shows Africa and the Arabian Peninsula. This is the part of the world in which baboons live.

The hamadryas baboon lives in Ethiopia, Eritrea, Somalia, Yemen, and Saudi Arabia. Hamadryas baboons were considered special by ancient Egyptians and were often shown in their art.

WHAT BABOONS EAT

Baboons are **omnivores**. This means they eat both plants and animals. Baboons will eat just about anything they can find. This is called being an opportunistic eater. They will eat fruits, tree bark, grasses, and other plant parts. They also eat meat, birds, fish, small **mammals**, and insects such as ants.

Most of a baboon's diet is fruits, vegetables, and other plants. Meat is generally harder for them to get. They eat it when they can, though.

When baboons get the chance, they will eat people's food, too. They have been known to eat crops, take food from kitchens, and kill farm animals such as sheep and goats. This makes baboons pests to many people.

ANTS

This is a chacma baboon in Cape Town, a city in South Africa. Here, wild baboons break into garbage cans and eat crops. They are sometimes seen as pests in the same way that raccoons and coyotes are pests in the United States.

IN THE TROOP

The baboon on the left is grooming the fur of the baboon on the right. Grooming helps build bonds between mates, mothers and babies, and other members of the troop.

Baboons live in troops, or groups. The savanna baboons live in troops that number up to hundreds of monkeys. The monkeys in these troops live under strict social rankings. The strongest male monkeys fight for control of the troop. The other monkeys follow the head baboon. The means that males' rankings may change during their lives. Females have the same rankings throughout their lives. These rankings come from their mothers. Relationships within a baboon troop are very important. Members spend hours every day bonding by grooming one another's fur. Baboons are quick to fight each other, though. They are known as the fiercest monkeys.

FUN FACT

Males sometimes use baby baboons to keep other males from fighting them. If a baby is hurt, the baby's mother and her family will join the fight. This generally keeps a baboon from starting a fight with a male holding a baby!

These chacma males are fighting one another. Males fight for rank in the troop, as well as over female mates.

15

MONKEYING AROUND

Baboons climb trees to find food and places to sleep. They spend most of the rest of their time on the ground, though. They play, **mate**, and spend time with other troop members on the ground. Baboons walk on all fours, using both their hands and their feet to get around.

Here you can see a troop of baboons traveling together. You can also see how these monkeys walk on all fours. This is called being quadrupedal.

FUN FACT

Older male baboons drop in social ranking as younger males fight their way up the ranking. Sometimes the younger baboons bully the older baboons until they leave and try to join another troop.

Baboons spend their days with the other monkeys in their troops. When they travel as a group, the high-ranking males are in the front, the females and young are in the middle, and the lower-ranking males are at the back. Baboons communicate within their troop and with other troops by making different sounds.

Baboons spend most of their time on the ground. They are able to climb trees, but they do not travel from tree to tree, as some monkeys do.

MALES AND FEMALES

Male baboons are generally larger than female baboons. An adult female baboon might be 20 inches (51 cm) tall, with a 1-foot-(30 cm) long tail, and weigh around 30 pounds (14 kg). An adult male baboon might be 30 inches (76 cm) tall, have a 2-foot-(61 cm) long tail, and weigh around 80 pounds (36 kg).

The female Guinea baboon on the right is caring for her young. A male (center) is standing behind her, and other troop members surround them.

Males court, or try to get females to mate with them, by bringing the females food, grooming them, and **protecting** them. The female will then pick the male with whom she wants to mate. The largest, strongest, and highest-ranking male baboons have the most success in finding females to mate with them.

Here is a male hamadryas baboon (left) with two females and a baby. In some troops each male has more than one female partner.

BABY BABOONS

Baby baboons grow inside their mothers for about six months. An adult female baboon generally gives birth to a baby every other year. She gives this baby all of her attention to teach it to take care of itself.

At birth, baboons have black or brown fur. The babies drink milk from their mothers

FUN FACT

Females stay with the same troop their whole lives. Males move to new troops when they reach adulthood.

The mother baboon does most of the parenting of the babies. Babies stay close to their mothers until they are about one year old.

20

for between 6 and 15 months. The mother also grooms and carries her baby. She teaches the baby the social rules of the troop and protects it from other baboons. The baby reaches adulthood at around five years of age. In the wild, baboons live to be around 30 years old.

This is a baby yellow baboon. As baby baboons grow, they start to add solid foods to their diets until they no longer need to drink their mothers' milk.

These are young olive baboons. As young baboons grow, they start to explore the world around them. Part of the way they do this is by playing with other baboons.

BABOONS AND PEOPLE

Lions, hyenas, and leopards are the baboons' wild **predators**. None of the baboon species are **endangered**, although baboon numbers near where people live are falling due to hunting and habitat loss.

Here is a group of yellow baboons at Hwange National Park, in Zimbabwe. National parks like this one help protect wild animal habitats.

In places where baboon troops live near cities or villages, baboons compete with people for land and water. People hunt baboons to protect their farms, homes, crops, and animals. There are groups that have set aside places for baboons to live. Scientists have also started to share information on how people can live more safely alongside these monkeys. Both of these things help keep people and baboons safe.

Glossary

canines (KAY-nynz) The pointy teeth that are on the side of the mouth and in front.

endangered (in-DAYN-jerd) In danger of no longer existing.

mammals (MA-mulz) Warm-blooded animals that have backbones and hair, breathe air, and feed milk to their young.

mate (MAYT) To come together to make babies.

New World (NOO WURLD) North America and South America.

Old World (OHLD WURLD) The part of the world that includes Asia, Africa, and Europe.

omnivores (OM-nih-vawrz) Animals that eat both plants and animals.

opposable (uh-POH-zuh-bel) Able to hold digits on a hand or foot together.

predators (PREH-duh-terz) Animals that kill other animals for food.

primates (PRY-mayts) The group of animals that are more advanced than others and includes monkeys, gorillas, and people.

protecting (pruh-TEKT-ing) Keeping safe.

savanna (suh-VA-nuh) A grassland with few trees or bushes.

species (SPEE-sheez) One kind of living thing. All people are one species.

tropical (TRAH-puh-kul) Having to do with the warm parts of Earth that are near the equator.

Index

A
Africa, 8, 10

F
feet, 6, 16
fur, 6, 15, 20

G
ground, 6, 16
group(s), 4, 14, 17

H
hands, 6, 16

M
males, 17, 19
mouth, 7
muzzle(s), 7

N
nose, 7
numbers, 22

O
omnivores, 12

P
palms, 6
people, 5, 13, 22
plains, 4
predators, 22
primates, 5

R
rankings, 14–15
relationships, 4, 15
relative, 5

S
savannas, 11
South America, 8
species, 6, 22

T
tails, 9, 18
teeth, 4, 7
thumbs, 9
troop(s), 4, 14–15, 17, 21–22

V
villages, 22

W
water, 22

Web Sites

Due to the changing nature of Internet links, PowerKids Press has developed an online list of Web sites related to the subject of this book. This site is updated regularly. Please use this link to access the list: www.powerkidslinks.com/monk/baboons/